NATIONAL GEOGRAPHIC
School Publishing

ROCK TOUR

PATHFINDER EDITION

By Beth Geiger

CONTENTS

ROCK TO

The United States has some amazing sights; vast caves, soaring rock towers, and jaw-dropping cliffs. Most took millions of years to form, and in some places, a climate different from today's helped create them. Rain or glaciers sculpted the land, changing ordinary places into spectacular ones, while in other spots, long-gone volcanoes had sizzling effects on the scenery. These forces helped put our rock stars on center stage.

Let's explore some these famous geologic wonders.

BY BETH GEIGER

Valley of Stars

Monument Valley, Utah, is not just for rock stars. The incredible scenery here has formed the backdrop for dozens of movies. Monument Valley is mostly made of a **sedimentary** rock called sandstone.

The sandstone formed slowly, as rivers, oceans, and wind spread thick layers of sand and other sediment. Over millions of years, the layers hardened into rock; then millions more years went by. The sandstone cracked and then weathering and erosion ate away at the layers.

Now, only delicate pillars and buttes with steep sides remain. A butte is a flat-topped mountain. These sedimentary rock formations rise over the desert.

Underground Wonders

Hidden under the New Mexico desert is a fairyland of vast rooms and shimmering shapes, called Carlsbad Caverns.

Carlsbad Caverns's Big Room is as big as 6.2 football fields! It's like a glittering palace with **Stalactites** that look like fangs hanging from the ceiling and delicate formations called soda straws and lily pads that glisten. The Big Room is just the beginning, though, because the cave stretches much farther.

Meeting in the Middle. Stalactites form from the ceiling of a cave, while stalagmites form from the floor, and where they meet, they form columns.

Like most big caves, Carlsbad Caverns is made of limestone, which is also a type of sedimentary rock. Limestone dissolves slowly in weak acids, and when rainwater seeps through the ground, it combines with carbon dioxide to make a weak acid. In Carlsbad Caverns, the acid water dissolved the rock, and then the dissolved minerals hardened into new shapes in new places. That's how Carlsbad Caverns's fantastic formations took shape.

Tree Tales

Dinosaurs once prowled through a lush forest in Arizona, but millions of years later, logs from the forest still lie on the ground. But don't bother looking for wood because the logs are made of rock! The place is now the Petrified Forest.

At the Petrified Forest, sand and soil buried fallen trees, and ash from nearby volcanoes covered the ground. Volcanic ash is full of minerals, and those minerals dissolved and seeped into the ground. After millions of years, the minerals replaced the wood, and the logs became stone. When wood turns to stone like this, it is called petrified.

Inside-Out Volcano

An inside-out volcano looms above the New Mexico desert. Some people thought it looked like a ragged old ship, so they named this pile of **igneous** rock Ship Rock.

Ship Rock didn't always stick up. Once it was a pipe under the ground that was filled with melted rock, which is called **magma**. Then a volcano rose above the pipe, and about 30 million years ago… kaboom! Magma from the pipe exploded from the volcano.

Afterward, the magma left in the pipe hardened into rock. Slowly, all the rock and soil around it wore away, but the magma didn't wear away. The pipe was left sticking up into the sky.

Tall Tower. Ship Rock is 600 meters (1,700 feet) high.

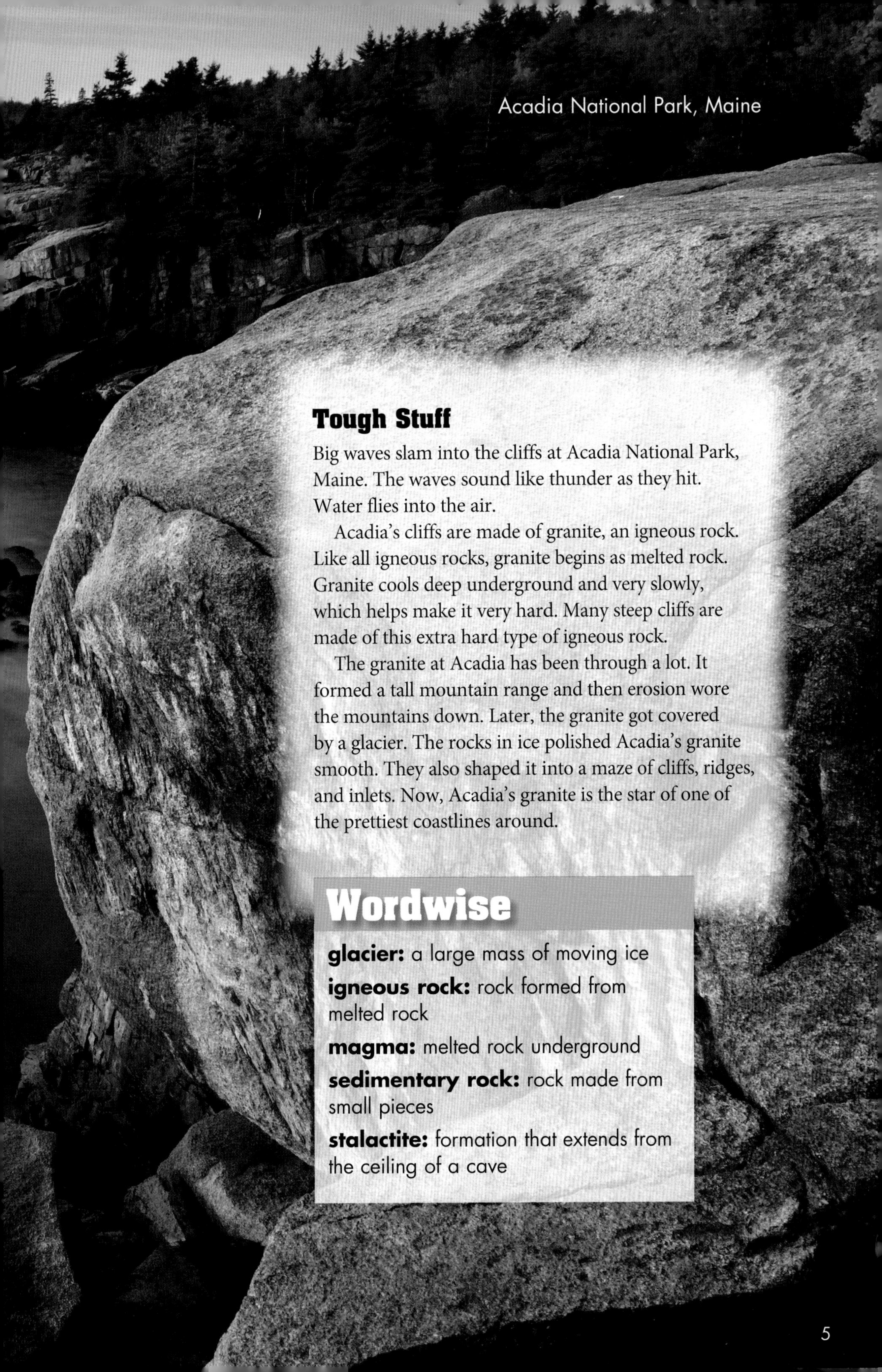

Acadia National Park, Maine

Tough Stuff

Big waves slam into the cliffs at Acadia National Park, Maine. The waves sound like thunder as they hit. Water flies into the air.

Acadia's cliffs are made of granite, an igneous rock. Like all igneous rocks, granite begins as melted rock. Granite cools deep underground and very slowly, which helps make it very hard. Many steep cliffs are made of this extra hard type of igneous rock.

The granite at Acadia has been through a lot. It formed a tall mountain range and then erosion wore the mountains down. Later, the granite got covered by a glacier. The rocks in ice polished Acadia's granite smooth. They also shaped it into a maze of cliffs, ridges, and inlets. Now, Acadia's granite is the star of one of the prettiest coastlines around.

Wordwise

glacier: a large mass of moving ice

igneous rock: rock formed from melted rock

magma: melted rock underground

sedimentary rock: rock made from small pieces

stalactite: formation that extends from the ceiling of a cave

ROCKIN' RECIPES

Oatmeal Raisin is just one type of cookie, and each rock shown is also just one type of sedimentary, igneous, or metamorphic rock.

Oatmeal Raisin Cookies

These oatmeal raisin cookies are made from different things, just like rocks.

Sedimentary Rock

Conglomerate rock is a type of sedimentary rock that's made of bits and pieces of other rocks.

Igneous Rock

Granite is a type of igneous rock. The rock is formed from minerals interlocked together.

Metamorphic Rock

Schist is a type of metamorphic rock. The bands and folds in the rock formed from pressure and heat.

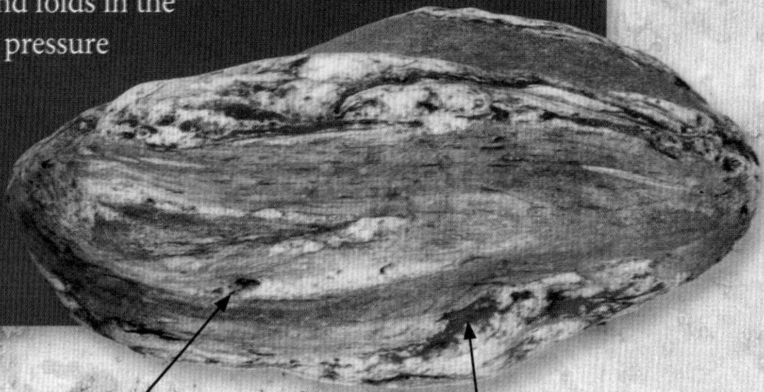

STAMPEDE!

"*Gold!*" thought carpenter John Marshall. He had just spotted something bright in a creek at Sutter's Mill, California, and sure enough, the yellow flakes were gold.

The date was January 24, 1848. By March, the news had spread like lightning. GOLD! People came to California from all over the world. The great Gold Rush was on!

The 49ers

Many of the gold seekers came in 1849, so they were nicknamed 49ers. Many 49ers found what they were looking for. Gold nuggets and flakes turned up in creeks all over California. Some bits of gold were very small. Others were as big as your fist…or even bigger.

Marshall's discovery changed California forever. People came for gold, and then they stayed.

Golden Cities. Cities like San Francisco grew from the gold rush.

Treasure of the Sierra Nevada

Sierra Nevada Mountains

The gold in California's creeks came from granite. The granite began as melted rock called magma. It was deep underground. Hot liquids mixed with the magma, and as the magma and liquids cooled, minerals and metals formed. One of those metals was gold. Not all granite has gold, but this granite had plenty.

Gradually, the rocks that covered the cooled granite wore away. The granite was exposed. It formed a tall mountain range, the Sierra Nevada mountains.

Over millions of years, rain, wind, and frost began to crumble the granite. Bits of rock washed into the streams that flow from the Sierra Nevada. So did the gold.

Mining for Gold. People probably found gold like this in Coloma, California. That's where the first gold was discovered.

No Ordinary Rock

Over time, wearing away moves ordinary rocks farther and farther from their source. The rocks break into smaller and smaller pieces. Gradually, they can be ground into sand.

But gold is different. First, it's heavier than most rocks. It settles quickly to the bottom of creeks. Big nuggets of gold don't wash very far downstream. What's more, gold doesn't break apart much. The flakes and nuggets stay whole.

While other rocks from the mountains washed towards the sea, gold collected in California's streams. It collected in cracks. The gold collected for millions of years.

Rough and Tumble

To get the gold, 49ers had to sort it from the gravel in the stream. First, they scooped up gravel and shook it in pans. Then they ran water over it to wash away the gravel. The heavy stuff settled out, and that was the gold.

Mining was hard work, and most miners never got rich. Sure, many found gold, but their savings disappeared quickly. The food and supplies they needed cost a fortune. In fact, the people who sold supplies to the miners were the ones who got rich!

Cleaning Up. When you wash away rocks and soil, the heavy gold is left behind.

Precious Metal. Necklaces like these are made with gold.

Good as Gold

Gold has a certain magic. People have treasured it for thousands of years.

What is so great about gold, anyway? It's rare, for one thing. That makes it valuable. Gold is softer than other metals. That makes it easy to shape into jewelry and coins. Gold doesn't tarnish or rust, so it stays shiny.

Gold is still precious today. It's useful, too. It's even used in computers.

Still There?

By about 1855, the California Gold Rush was over. Most of the gold that was easy to find was gone. The 49ers moved on and mining companies moved in. They dug deeper into the granite to find more gold.

The Sierra Nevada mountains haven't worn away yet. They are still tall and beautiful. Trails lead into wild, rocky valleys. Lakes sparkle under granite cliffs. Is there still gold in some of the granite? Naturally!

Rock Tour

Answer these rockin' questions to see what you've learned about rocks.

1. Why do you think many of Monument Valley's buttes have flat tops?
2. How does igneous rock form?
3. What makes granite so hard?
4. How did gold get into the streams near the mountains?
5. Why would gold sink down to the bottom of streams?